What Do I Do When...
My Child Won't Do As I Say?

BY POLLY GREENBERG

Illustrations by James Hale

Copyright © 1996 by Sch
Illustrations copyright © 1996 ⌐
All rights reserved. Published by Scholastic inc.
Printed in the U.S.A.
ISBN 0-590-89926-0

11 12 13 14 15 16 17 18 19 20   05 06 07

D0003219

DEDICATION

To my super daughter Liza,
the only one of my five grown daughters
(four of whom are wonderful parents)
who has never had a single
discipline problem. (That's because she
hasn't yet had her children.)

Table of Contents

Introduction

Your child needs firm discipline daily.

Cute kindergartner Tim complains that his mother makes him brush his teeth. Classmate Max, an adorable but seriously neglected child, says wistfully, "I wish my mother would make *me* brush my teeth. She doesn't even care if I *have* any teeth."

Kindly discipline makes children feel secure and cared for.

The most effective discipline consists of:

- **friendly, flexible guidelines to live by**
- **reasonable routines**
- **age-appropriate behavioral standards**
- **a good example.**

Of course, being a good example is the hardest part — and perhaps the most important. That's because who we are has much more impact upon who our children will become than does any technique we use in raising and disciplining them.

To discipline means to provide guidance that encourages cooperative, acceptable behavior whenever it's needed:

- **throughout the day**
- **throughout all the days of childhood and adolescence.**

(That's why disciplining can get truly tiresome!)

If you are a basically good person, your child has a head start on becoming a good person. And, after all is said and done, that is the goal of child-rearing.

Disciplining is an ongoing process of teaching your child to become a more cooperative person who, more and more each year, can discipline herself.

Discipline That's Fun, Friendly, and Firm

As every parent knows, babies are not all born alike. Maybe yours was an easy baby with a calm temperament. Or maybe your infant was "difficult" — more sensitive or irritable. And as every parent also knows, children are not all equally easy to live with. Not all three- to seven-year-olds are equally cooperative. Not all react equally well to fair, friendly requests. Some young children are definitely more difficult to deal with than others. Some children are downright defiant.

Whatever a child's temperament, it is our goal as parents to gently but firmly guide him or her toward being an okay person. Blaming the genetics your baby was born with won't help, even though it is part of the

Begin With "Friendly"

Whether you want to

- **improve the way you provide "development guidance"**

or

- **design a "remedial routine" to correct behavioral wrongs, strengthening your friendship with each of your children is a primary piece of the process. (See suggestions on p. 30.)**

picture. Genetics, parenting, and other environmental factors intertwine in subtle ways. The part you can best control is the parenting.

All effective discipline, even for the most difficult child, is based on — is part of — a caring, considerate, comfortable relationship.

Your life at home — your circumstances, your relationships — also figure into disciplining your child.

By the time a child is just three years old — not to mention seven years old — she has experienced a great deal of her family's life.

Have you been able to make friends with your child? To respond to many of her wants and all of her needs?

Have you gently, and with a bit of jollying, set limits for her, helping her learn how to "act right"?

What is your life like apart from your child? Feeling very worried and wearied by adult stresses can make it hard to muster the will and patience to pursue the plan of discipline you want for your child.

Still, as long as your child is loved by at least one person, and as long as your family, whatever form it takes, is fundamentally okay, then fun, friendly, firm discipline is possible for you.

Relieve Your Stress

If undue stress is interfering with your ability to parent, you'll likely benefit from professional counseling and support services — and/or rearranging your life to permit more sleep. (Ah, sleep, that magic, often-forgotten elixir that makes patient parenting possible!)

What's Happening for You?

Your attitude about discipline is an essential part of making it work. Check off any of the following comments that echo your own feelings.

1. Frequently, I feel completely defeated by my child. ☐

2. Sometimes I feel so frustrated that I'm afraid I might lose it. It seems like my child almost never does anything I say. ☐

3. My parents were extremely strict. I vowed that I would never treat my children so unfairly and harshly! But they don't obey me at all. ☐

4. My child argues nonstop. I spend half my day debating and making deals with him. ☐

5. We are doing more spanking than we would like to, but we do believe in discipline. ☐

6. I think children should do what they are told to do without a lot of fuss. ☐

7. Often, I find myself shrieking and screaming at my child. I hate myself when I do it, yet I think my child should do as I say. ☐

8. My wife lets our children do just about whatever they want. I want well-behaved children. ☐

9. I was raised very permissively, so I am having trouble being a disciplinarian. ☐

10. My child won't obey me, even in an emergency. ☐

Did you check some or most of items 1, 2, 3, 4, 9, and 10?

If so, may I have a word with you?

You don't have to be mean and punitive to have a child who behaves "well enough." You do have to feel that you're the boss and set clear standards. You do have to stick to your word and carry out consequences if your child chooses not to adhere to your standards. You won't have to administer negative consequences often if your child learns that you mean what you say.

If you are on the verge of "losing it," seek help. Call a local parenting hot line or support services.

Did you check some or most of items 5, 6, 7, and 8?

If so, you may want to consider this: Mainstream child psychologists, early childhood educators, and parenting specialists believe in firm discipline and well-behaved children.

If you answered yes to some of the questions (and it's hard to imagine a parent who wouldn't!), you might want to try the approach to child guidance explained in this little book for six months. Then compare. Are things going better between you and your child?

Discipline
in an
Emergency

Let's consider extreme situations. Your child must obey instantly in an emergency.

A distraught father told me that when his son was in the middle of the street, possibly about to be hit, instead of instantly moving as directed, the five-year-old tried to engage in debate and discussion. The dad said, "Even at a time like that, he challenges my authority!"

Once, when my own children were very young, I had the "littles," aged two and three, in a bath. The "bigs" were playing elsewhere. Suddenly I smelled smoke!

Leaving the kids alone in the tub for the first time in their lives, I galloped downstairs, saw flames, and raced back up, yelling, "Big girls! It's an emergency! Each of you get a sister out of the tub! Hurry outside! Stay there!" Then I immediately called the fire department.

Hurrying outside myself, I saw my four little children

excitedly watching fire engines arrive.

"You are so good!" I laughed, encircling them all in a bear hug. "How did you get so good?"

"You said it was a 'mergency," the six-year-old replied matter-of-factly. "We know what to do when you say that: stop, listen, do what we're told quickly. Talk about it later."

"We trained the 'littles' to do that," the five-year-old said proudly. "So they did it right, too."

Prepare for Emergencies

1 Avoid giving an avalanche of instructions every day. Giving continual orders immunizes children against registering any of them.

2 Allow your children lots of opportunities for independence and initiative in play and in suitable decision-making (Dress before or after breakfast? Peas, carrots, or both?). Intrusive, overbearing parents often produce resistant, defiant children.

3 Explain that once in a while something scary or dangerous might be about to happen. Explain that it's your job to protect your children. Tell them what to do if you ever say, "It's an emergency!"

4 Establish a sensible, practical discipline system in your family. (The rest of this book may help.) Soon you'll see your children assisting you in implementing it when you need it most!

Transitions –
Invitations to Misbehave

Terry tells me that *all* of her children give her fits on and off during each day.

"They can't shift gears from one thing to another," Terry frets. "Especially Eddie. Eddie pushes my buttons. I'm efficient. I want to move swiftly through my day. But Eddie! He's a very intense little boy. Whatever he's doing, he's deeply into it. We can't get him to switch to what needs to be done next."

Some children *are* much less adaptable than others. I guess Eddie is one of them.

Yet your child, like every child, must endure many changes and waits (transitions) throughout the day. And your child, like every child, probably has trouble with transitions.

Here are some suggestions I gave Terry. She reports that they've helped quite a bit. "Now the kids are much more likely to do what I say, and sooner," she says.

Create a schedule for your day:

■ Unreasonable rigidity breeds blowups and dares dawdlers (dawdling is such a disruptive and powerful form of resistance!). But having no schedule breeds chaos.

■ The routines embedded in a daily schedule provide security — they give young children a protected, safely surrounded feeling.

■ An important part of positive self-esteem is the ability to predict what's about to happen. A schedule provides children with many opportunities to predict and, therefore, to prepare emotionally.

■ Children need many chances each day to feel intelligent and competent. The less they feel like puppets being led by the strings you pull and the more they feel that they have the information they need to do some self-management, the easier transition times will usually be — that is, the more likely it is that your child will do as you say.

Reduce the number of transitions in your schedule as much as you can.

■ Creating large blocks of playtime, framed by necessary routines and errands, eliminates the need to interrupt children so much. Then you can explain to your dawdler that you are cooperating with his need for time to do what he wants and you need him to cooperate with what you need too.

■ Your child is naturally active, busy, talkative — and a slowpoke when you want him to hurry. Young children are leisure-lovers. This makes it difficult to move them through the many transitions in a typical day. To the extent possible, stretch the time you allow in your schedule for "finishing up," "putting your coat on," and so forth, to accommodate your child's turtlelike pace. If you expect slowness and plan time for it, it won't be so aggravating.

Get your child's attention and prepare him for changes.

■ Frequently, when a child protests, "But I didn't hear you!" after you say he isn't doing as you told him, he really didn't hear you. First, get his attention. Put your hand on his shoulder, and look into his eyes. It's easier for any of us to pay attention if our mind isn't on something else.

■ For your child, abruptly stopping play is the same as leaving a job unfinished. Give your child a few minutes to reach "closure" on what he's doing. A good rule of thumb is a three-minute warning for a three-year-old, a six-minute warning for a six-year-old, and so forth. "In three minutes, we're going to Aunt Annie's, so finish up your building, Sam." (Younger children only know about "now," so a longer wait is too long; older children's play is more involved, so they need more time to finish.)

Keep instructions simple and cheerful — if feasible, be funny.

■ "Get your lunch box, yum-yum-yum, yo-ho-ho, it's time to go."

■ "Shoes. On feet." Point to shoes, point to feet.

■ "You can't find your jacket? I can find your jacket! It's covering your head, silly!" (Toss the jacket over your child's head, laughing as you help her into it.)

Keep waits infrequent, brief, and fun-filled.

Let's face it, children are very poor waiters.

■ Plan ahead so that when they're ready, you're ready.

■ Have a few songs, stories, or fingerplays in mind, or fool around and joke with your kiddies.

One thing is for sure: Children get into trouble when they have to hurry up and wait.

Think of all the changes and waiting your child must endure!

■ moving from dreamland to daytime

■ getting to breakfast

■ waiting for the food

■ getting dressed, teeth brushed, etc.

■ waiting for help when needed

■ getting ready to leave for child care or school

■ waiting for you or another grown-up to take him there

■ getting settled at child care or school

■ saying goodbye

■ a daily schedule of classroom transitions

■ getting ready to leave

■ waiting for you or another grown-up to take him home

■ waiting for you to have time for him (to tell you something, to get something for him, to help him, to play with him)

■ maybe waiting for you to come home from work

■ stopping play to clean up

- stopping cleaning up to go to dinner

- getting to dinner

- waiting for the food

- getting back to playing or watching or working

- getting undressed, teeth brushed, etc.

- waiting for help when needed

- getting ready to "leave" you (by falling asleep)

And anytime anyone comes or goes, your child is forced to adjust! This, too, is an emotional transition!

Change the Pace

To your child, many of the little switches — which you scarcely notice — from one thing to the next on the agenda are major interruptions and irritations. Your child will probably feel more cooperative if:

1 You allow for her need:
- to be engrossed in activity
- to be able to predict and feel competent/independent
- for a leisurely life pace.

2 You prepare her for changes — and ensure that your instructions are really heard.

3 You use fun-filled guidance to help you both function with less friction.

How to Establish Your
Authority

Invest time in planning. You'll reap many rewards.

1 **Brainstorm.** List all the examples you can of exactly what your child does that irritates you because she doesn't do as you ask.

2 **Rank the annoying behaviors.** Some irritating behaviors are less irksome than others. Decide which behaviors are worth making an issue over. Can you look the other way and let some of the less serious disobedience go?

3 **Learn to laugh.** Many wrong things that children do can be viewed as funny, if you get yourself in the right mood. Laughing it off (another way of turning the other cheek) is sometimes more suitable than agonizing over sober "behavior-modification strategies."

4 **Face the harsh truth:** you'll never be a perfect parent. Not today, not tomorrow, not ever. Moreover, your child will never be a perfect child. So give your child and yourself permission to sometimes fumble, and occasionally fail.

5 **Worry less, and enjoy more.** Delight in the innocence, the hugs, the kisses, the *good* stuff kids do.

6 **Reward the right stuff.** Throughout the day, when your child is doing okay (nothing wrong), blow him a kiss, smile and wave, toss him a compliment about how well he is playing or how great he's being. Once in a while, surprise him with a small gift.

7 **If there are two of you** (mom and dad, mother and grandmother — any two), you may not agree on which behaviors are most distressing. Now's the time to discuss, disagree, compromise, and decide on your campaign so you'll usually come across to the kids as consistent and united.

8 **Consider whether the behavior is building "bad character"** or is just a silly childhood thing that the child will outgrow. If your six-year-old won't stop being cruel to others and to animals, it's much more alarming than if she won't stop making silly noises at dinner. Sort it out and agree to go after only the serious problems in a serious way. Perhaps you can give lesser problems less rigorous attention for now.

9 **Can you agree to disagree, but to support each other's top priorities?** Dad can't stand back talk, but doesn't much mind dawdling. Mom can't stand dawdling, but sassiness doesn't much bother her. For the sake of effective discipline (and a happy marriage), can you back each other up?

10 **Move from** "I can't do a thing with him!" and "You won't get away with this, young man!" to united and empowered parenting. When you *know* you are in charge, your child will know it, too.

When Your Child
Won't Listen

My friend Hannah has one of the most disobedient six-year-olds I know. The child acts like a horrendous pest. She clamors and climbs on her mother throughout any conversation her mom is having with another adult. She gets into things the way we expect toddlers to — but this girl is six!

In fact, she acts like a toddler in general. What's normal for toddlers and twos in the way of oppositional behavior (doing the opposite of what you say), should not be typical of six-year-olds.

I feel sorry for my friend. She sees other parents with their children. She sees that by three and a half, children usually do what adults tell them to, if we are tactful and reasonable.

But her daughter, Sara, doesn't quit even when Hannah, red-faced and frustrated to the nth degree, shouts, "No! Stop!"

Time Sample of Sara's Misbehavior

12:00 At the lunch table, Sara kneels and reaches for sugar. Hannah asks her to stop. Sara pokes fingers in sugar bowl, pours sugar on table, plays in it as if it were sand. Hannah continues talking with me.

12:02 Sara interrupts me. Hannah shushes her. Sara continues to talk, repeating herself over and over. Hannah talks over her voice.

12:04 Sara starts thunderously kicking the leg of the table. Hannah pleads with her to stop. Sara keeps kicking. Also now whines the words she was saying before.

12:05 Sara shakes salt into her milk. Hannah now shouts, "No! Stop!" Sara stirs milk vigorously so it slops over, then shakes salt on table.

12:06 Sara taps spoon on glass — louder, louder, louder. Hannah shouts again, "No! Stop!" Sara continues the clear, ringing taps.

12:07 Sara launches into a whiny harangue about why she deserves extra dessert.

12:09 Looking flustered and embarrassed, Hannah cuts her two pieces of cake.

Shouting urgently should cause any child to stop immediately. Hannah is horribly embarrassed.

Half an hour eating lunch with Hannah and Sara proves to me without a doubt why this child (who loves her mother very much) ignores her mom. (See "Time Sample of Sara's Misbehavior," above.)

"See what I mean?" my friend says to me after this interchange. "She always argues. She ignores what I say. I'm raising a brat." Hannah glares at the child.

"I do see what you mean," I say. You are raising a brat, I think.

I do feel sorry for

Hannah because I know she wants desperately to be a good mom, and because to some extent or another all parents know what it feels like to be humiliated by their child's behavior.

But I also find this fascinating. Without realizing it, Hannah has taught her daughter to ignore her words, even urgent words.

- **Hannah ignores Sara's bad behavior until it gets on her nerves too much. Then she shouts ineffectively.**

- **She doesn't explain what she wants Sara to do (sit still, eat neatly, listen and take turns talking as grown-ups do).**

- **She doesn't remind Sara of what she expects.**

- **She doesn't warn of a consequence that will result from bad behavior.**

- **She never follows through with a consequence.**

Let's help Hannah find a way out. But first, a little first aid!

If your child isn't doing as you ask:

1 Politely tell your child what you want her to do.

2 Politely remind her once.

3 Give a warning — mention a consequence that will follow if she chooses not to cooperate with what you've asked her to do.

4 Do what you said you would do.

Hope for Hannah:
Parents Can Learn New Tricks

All of us tend to parent as we were parented — or the opposite way, as a swing-of-the-pendulum reaction to parenting we weren't happy with.

If you were parented in a predominantly polite, respectful yet firm manner, if you were guided through the normal misbehaviors of a typical childhood, then positive child guidance probably comes more or less naturally for you.

However, if your parents were excessively harsh, or neglectful by not noticing and guiding your behavior, you may not feel confident that you know what to do. (As if anyone does!)

Hannah may be doing a version of what her parents did — sometimes they weren't aware of her at all, no matter what she did, and at other times they shouted and roared at her ineffectually. They had little idea of what to expect of their child at each age and stage. Hannah is in the same situation. That's why her six-year-old acts like a toddler. Hannah hates the mess she's in, but feels helpless.

There is hope. Children can learn and parents can too! Hannah — and you — can gain new knowledge and try new approaches to old (oh-so-old) problems — approaches that effectively teach your child "to do what I say."

Four Steps to
Better Behavior

Here's an approach to child guidance that works with most young children (aged three and up) most of the time. (You can sometimes use it with younger children, but generally you need more preventive measures and less talk — and lower expectations to match their abilities.)

The four-step approach:

- **prevents behavior problems from developing and becoming persistent**

- **increases in firmness and sternness, in a step-by-step way, when your child resists.**

This escalating sequence of steps nips in the bud, or eventually conquers, most common behavior problems.

Hannah's daughter, Sara, from the previous pages, is well-practiced at ignoring communications from her mother. So we don't imagine that she will respond at first to the early steps in this sequence. Nonetheless, to help her learn and to be fair to Sara, we start with Step 1 before we escalate.

The sequence starts with

the least amount of parent power. Assume that your young child loves you, knows she needs you, wants to please you, and is, at heart, a reasonable little person. Assume that good behavior is best taught by an adult setting an example of good behavior — showing self-control and a respectful way of speaking to people (including children). Think about it: Do you want your child to get red in the face and shout angrily at people? Then we parents best not do it either.

THE STEPS:

Start by communicating clearly.

1 Politely, simply, and as positively as possible, state what it is that you expect.

When you speak, say your child's name first, to get her attention. Follow the name with exactly what you want her to do.

"Sara, I expect you to sit down when we're having a meal together. Sit your bottom down on your chair."

(If she sits, Sara won't be able to fool around with the sugar bowl.)

2 Give your child a second reminder.

■ Try saying her name, catching her eye, and giving her "that look"
or
■ Say her name and raise your eyebrows in disapproval while clearing your throat
or
■ Put your hand on her shoulder, say her name, and frown.

Most of us parents talk way too much. (Not Sara's mother, she has a different problem: failure to follow through.) We need more effective techniques and less verbiage. Sometimes these nonverbal, more physical messages do the trick with less talk.

3 Follow one request and one reminder with a warning. A warning is a statement of the consequence if non-compliance continues.

"Sara, if you continue to climb around and mess with the sugar or do anything else that isn't appropriate when we're eating together, you'll finish your lunch in another room where your behavior won't bother us."

But if you say it, be prepared to do it, even if you have to carry your child away kicking and screaming.

4 Implement your "promise." Remove your child.

If, by any chance, your child should refuse to stay "removed," and returns uninvited, remove her again. And again. And again. As often as needed.

NOTE: Hannah began using escalating parent power, and it worked! At our next lunch, Hannah was able to stop Sara's behavior well before it became bratty.

Stick to It!

When children are raised with these clear steps to discipline used consistently from age three, it's seldom necessary to enforce a consequence.

Words
That Work

Children are more willing to do what we ask if we phrase things positively. Your child is likely to cooperate better with your requests if you use the tried-and-true wording in the column on the left, rather than the negative wording in the column on the right.

WORDS THAT WORK	WORDS THAT DON'T
Show that you recognize and accept the reason the child is doing the "wrong thing":	Avoid just stating what you want the child to do without showing that you understand her viewpoint:
■ "You want to play with the glass bowl, but…"	■ "Get away from that bowl. You'll break it!"
■ "You want me to sleep with you all night but…"	■ "I don't want to sleep with you! I have my own bed!"
Offer acceptable choices, not just *no*'s:	Avoid unaccompanied *no*'s. It's hard for children to accept them when it seems that's all they ever hear.
■ "We can't go outside now, but you can use your clay or blocks if you want to."	■ "No! I said no!"

Behavior Talks –
Learn the Language

D oes your child ever fail to put her shoes on when it's time to go to school? Or "need" a drink of water again and again after bedtime? Burst into tears for what seems like no reason? Have you ever thought about why your child does these things?

Young children send messages through their behavior. They aren't always adept enough with language to explain their physical, emotional, social, or intellectual needs in words. So they act them out.

■ Physical

A hungry and tired child may be whiny and may easily "lose it." She isn't likely to say, "Dad, I'm exhausted, so

I've lost my self-control." But you can teach her to say what's bothering her; that's a good goal.

■ Emotional

A stressed and anxious child may be clingy, have nightmares, and throw tantrums. He isn't likely to say, "Man, I'm frantic with fear because you guys are getting divorced." But you can encourage him to reveal his feelings and fears, and can be reassuring.

Social

A child who has no peer to play with day after day may make excessive demands upon a parent or grandma to play with him. Or he may climb the walls and drive you nuts. He isn't likely to say, "Hey, folks, I need someone my age to be silly with and to set up a space station on the sofa with." But you can fan his self-awareness.

Intellectual

A child who lacks playthings (which can be branches and rocks as well as toys and games) or who lacks interesting stories, projects, outings, and conversation may get into trouble for lack of anything better to do with her brain and imagination. She isn't likely to say "The reason I'm tearing up this place is that I don't have opportunities to challenge my mind if I choose to." But you can help her interpret her feelings.

A key to effective discipline is to become a good observer of children, one who listens with a "third ear" to the probable meanings of their behavior and is sensitive to their needs.

You can:

- **prevent many problems by listening when your child communicates verbally or through behavior**

- **respond promptly and appropriately**

- **help your child learn words with which to explain feelings.**

What Is Your Child Telling You?
Some Possible Translations

THE BEHAVIOR:

Your child delays and dawdles when departure for her child-care center or school is imminent. You ask her to hurry, but she won't.

What Could This Mean?

Possibly your child is saying, "I love you, I like being home with you. I wish I didn't have to go away all day."

What Might You Feel?

■ You may have been feeling angry at your balky child. Now you may feel guilty!

■ There's no need to feel guilty if you've chosen a center staffed by friendly, caring teachers. There's no need to feel guilty if you check with your child and her teacher from time to time to make sure that her school experiences are going well.

What Can You Do?

Respond to the message your child may be sending you. Say things like:

■ "I like to be with you. I like us to be together. What should we do together when we get home from work and school?"

■ "It's hard to leave each other, isn't it? You have your special place to go and I have mine, but later we'll be together again. I'm going to grow a great big hug for you all day long. I hope you'll grow me a huge, soft hug."

THE BEHAVIOR:

Your child resists your every command. You are brusque and businesslike; he is rude and rebellious.

What Could This Mean?

Maybe your son is saying, "I'm not a high-speed superman like you. I'm just a little boy. I can't follow so many marching orders. I need more time and more choices."

What Might You Feel?

▪ You may have been feeling competitive with your child. Try being creative!

▪ How many suitable choices and decisions can you think of for him to make? How can his drive toward independence be given constructive outlets so he doesn't have to show his independence by doing what you don't want him to?

What Can You Do?

Respond to the message your child may be sending you. Say things like:

▪ "You're a smart guy. I like your ideas. Let's think about this: How can we solve this problem?" Listen to your child's ideas respectfully.

▪ "It seems like you don't always want to do as I say. Let's figure out some things that you can decide for yourself and some things that you will cooperate and do because I need you to. Let's be partners and work this out."

How to Enrich Your Friendship With Your Child

Fun, friendly, and firm discipline is built on a foundation of friendship. Here are some tips for building a rich and rewarding relationship with your child:

1 Stop (at least briefly) when your child is talking to you.

Look, listen, and respond. We all appreciate being listened to.

2 Eat dinner together almost every night.

Yes, everyone has a frenzied schedule. But this is part of the problem. It takes time to grow good kids. Concentrate on conversation. Deal with manners and healthy eating habits, but don't dwell on these nuts and bolts. Get to know each other!

3 Take a quick look now and then when your child is playing.

Make an appreciative comment: "That's interesting!" "Hey, looks like you have a good idea there!" "You seem to be having fun!"

4 Follow your child's lead.

If your child is withdrawn, moody, or oppositional and

would react to remarks like those above by saying, "Don't talk to me!" then don't. Just sit on the fringes of the play for a few minutes. Try for eye contact, accompanied by a knowing smile or wink — a friendly gesture, a warm family connection.

5 **Notice your child's individual interest.**
Look for opportunities to help expand what she is doing: Give her aluminum foil from which to form tiny dishes for the doll house people, a piece of hose to add reality to the firefighter play.

6 **Find 15 minutes or more of private time to be with each of your children every day.**
Together, put the appointment on the calendar. Tell your child how much you're looking forward to it. Do something he especially likes: Make pudding, play his favorite music, do a puzzle, play in the bath. (This is also an excellent soother and bond-builder with a difficult child.)

7 **Read (or look through) the bedtime story of your child's choice every night.**
Even primary-grade children enjoy a good read (perhaps from a library book) and a few cozy minutes with a parent.

Endnote

If you are like most parents, you are extremely busy doing all the things you must do and all the things you think you should do for your children. But unless we choose to, we do not have to hurtle through our children's childhood, seldom getting a chance to enjoy them.

Enrichments and lessons enhance children's lives up to a point, until they begin to rob children of ample opportunity to hang out, be with their families, and just enjoy life.

One of the most valuable gifts you can give your children is a relaxed, happy childhood, filled with affectionate encouragement and grounded in fun, friendly, and firm guidance. Every child needs at least one adult who spends some leisurely time with him — and *believes* in him.

Polly Greenberg